LET'S TALK ABOUT THE JEWISH HOLIDAYS

LET'S TALK ABOUT THE JEWISH HOLIDAYS

By
DOROTHY K. KRIPKE

Illustrated by
NAAMA KITOV

JONATHAN DAVID PUBLISHERS
New York

LET'S TALK ABOUT THE JEWISH HOLIDAYS
Copyright 1970 1981
by
DOROTHY K. KRIPKE

Paperback Edition 1981
ISBN 0-8246-0267-6

1989 1988

10 9 8 7 6 5 4

No part of this book may be reproduced in any form without the prior written consent of Jonathan David Publishers.

Library of Congress Catalogue Card No. 75-104328

Printed in the United States of America

*For Ned and Joan and Elizabeth,
For Sandy and Ned,
And for Susan and David and Daniel,
Who share my joy in
The Jewish holidays.*

TABLE OF CONTENTS

	Prologue *Which Only Means a Few Words Beforehand*	1
I	Rosh HaShanah *The Birthday of the World*	3
II	Yom Kippur *Making Friends With God*	7
III	Sukkot *The Time of Our Happiness*	11
IV	Simchat Torah *A Proud Parade*	15
V	Chanukkah *A Wonderful Thing Happened There*	19
VI	Tu BiShevat *Trees Have a Holiday*	23
VII	Purim *It Happened in Persia*	27
VIII	Pesach *The Time of Our Freedom*	31
IX	The Seder *The Dinner That is Food For Thought*	35
X	Israel Independence Day *A Dream Come True*	39
XI	Shavuot *When the World Held Its Breath*	43
XII	Tisha B'Av *A People Weeps*	47
	Epilogue *Which Only Means a Few Words Afterwards*	51

PROLOGUE

Which Only Means a Few Words Beforehand

Holidays are jewel days
That sparkle through the year.
When one has passed in peace and joy
Another one is near.

HAVE YOU EVER thought about the Jewish holidays and asked yourself the question, "Which of our holidays do I like best?"

"Oh," you will probably answer, "that's easy." Some will say Chanukkah; others will say Pesach; and still others will say Purim. Perhaps you will think of a different holiday.

So, you see, it is not such an easy question to answer. Not if you really think about each holiday.

There is a holiday that comes every week, the Sabbath. But we will talk only about the once-a-year holidays. Let us, then, spend a little time in talking about our holidays.

ROSH HASHANAH, our New Year, usually comes in September. Long ago our people imagined this was the birthday of the world.

Birthdays are jolly days. Holidays, too, are happy days as well as holy days. Indeed, the Hebrew way of saying holiday is *Yom Tov*, which means "a good day." So, Rosh HaShanah is a happy time. But even more it is a holy time, for it is the Day of Judgment.

The Day of Judgment is a time when we feel as though we are on trial before a Judge who knows everything about us. At the same time we feel as though we judge ourselves too. Long ago, our people, who had wonderful imaginations, said that it was as though God had a great big book in which were written the name and deeds of every person, and that this book told what would happen to each person in the year that was about to begin. Since no person is perfect, and since each of us does the wrong thing sometimes, it is lucky for us that God is very willing to forgive our wrong deeds.

A prayer that we say in the synagogue on Rosh HaShanah and again on Yom Kippur tells us there are three things we must do if we want God to forgive us. We must be truly sorry for the wrong things we have done. (This means, of course, that we will really try not to do the same wrong things again.) We must pray from our hearts and really mean it. And we must try to help other people.

This prayer, and others too, makes us feel how holy and important the holiday is. And the strange, mysterious, wonderful sound of the *shofar*, which we hear during the synagogue service, makes us feel this too.

At home there are greeting cards from family and friends to wish us a healthy, happy, good New Year. There are special treats, cookies and honey cakes, wine and delicious foods. At dinner, the *challah* is round. We dip slices of it into honey. Just as honey is sweet, we hope there will be sweet, good things happening for us in the new year.

The holiday feels very holy and important. We ourselves feel very important too. We know that each of us is only a tiny part of a great big world. But at the very same time, we know how important we are. Many of us like Rosh HaShanah especially because it gives us this special feeling.

THE HOLY DAY of Yom Kippur comes very soon after Rosh HaShanah. These two holidays together are called the High Holy Days, because they are so important. Indeed, Yom Kippur, the Day of Atonement, is the most important day of the Jewish year.

Before Yom Kippur there is a feeling of preparing for something very special and of waiting for something very important to happen.

Dinner is early, while it is still very light outside. Half an hour or so before the sun sets, grown-ups begin to fast. And the fasting goes on until it is dark the next night. The people who fast eat no food at all and drink no water or anything else until Yom Kippur is over. And, of course, there is no cooking or working of any kind on this holy day.

Before the fast begins candles are lit. Then the family goes to the synagogue for the Yom Kippur Eve service. Often, people dress in white, for white means purity. Our prayers

will tell God that we are truly sorry for the wrong things we have done in the old year and that we will really try to do better in the new year. Then God will forgive us, and we will be pure, like our white clothes.

On Yom Kippur Eve and through the day, we spend many hours in the synagogue. There are beautiful prayers, many of them special for the High Holy Days. Over and over again, we tell God how sorry we are for the wrong things we have done. And we know that if we really mean it, God will forgive us.

As the sun begins to set on Yom Kippur day, our prayers seem faster and faster and deeper and deeper. It is almost as though there are gates in heaven that are closing, and we must hurry to get our prayers in. Our hearts beat a little faster and there is a feeling of excitement in the air. At the end of the service, the *shofar* is sounded—one long, hopeful call—and Yom Kippur is over.

We wish our family and friends a good year. Then we hurry home to break our fast, to eat and drink for the first time in more than a day.

Yom Kippur, the Day of Atonement, is not a jolly holiday and not even an easy one. And yet, some of us consider it a kind of favorite, because, inside ourselves, Yom Kippur makes us feel so clean and shiny and brand new. It makes us feel lighter all over. We feel as though we have "made friends" with God. We are "at one" with God. And this is what we mean when we say that Yom Kippur is the Day of *At-one-ment*, the Day of Atonement.

10

3 SUKKOT
THE TIME OF OUR HAPPINESS

In my Sukkah I can see
The harvest moon shine down on me.
Then thanks, O God, I give to Thee
For fruit of vine and fruit of tree.

JUST A FEW DAYS after Yom Kippur comes Sukkot. The Bible tells us, "Be happy on your holiday." And, indeed, we are.

In the few days between Yom Kippur and Sukkot, we have built and decorated our *Sukkah*. This is a little hut outside the house. It has walls, but no roof. Instead of a roof there are branches or cornstalks to cover the top. Through these we can see the blue sky by day and the round, bright yellow moon at night.

In the Land of Israel, it is autumn, and the air is cool and crisp. The autumn leaves, all gold and brown and rusty-red, dance in the breeze and wave good-bye to the trees. Although, for two thousand years now, most Jews have lived in other lands, many of our holidays still depend on the seasons of the land where our people and its holidays started, the Land of Israel. Where we live it may be autumn, or it may be spring. It doesn't matter. In Israel, on Sukkot, it is autumn and harvest time, time to gather the ripe fruits. So, wherever we live, Sukkot is a harvest holiday.

As evening comes and Sukkot starts, Mother lights the candles in the *Sukkah*. Father chants *Kiddush* over a cup of wine. Then everyone sits down and says a blessing about sitting-in-the-*Sukkah*. Indeed, we thank God for all His blessings.

We thank God every day for His blessings. But Sukkot especially is a Thanksgiving holiday. We thank God for keeping us alive. Be-

cause it is autumn in Israel, fruits that grow from trees and vines are now ripe. For these, too, we thank God, for yellow pears and purple plums and blue-black grapes.

We thank God for the things that grow. So, we have a special blessing over the *etrog*, which looks very like a lemon, and the *lulav*, which is made from branches of palms and certain other growing things. We are really thanking God for all growing things.

The *Sukkah* makes us think of many things. Sometimes, as we sit in the *Sukkah*, a whistling wind whirls right through and makes us shiver. Sometimes it rains, and everything gets wet and drippy. Then, we realize that life is like the *Sukkah*. There are times when the sun disappears and there are only dark clouds and rain—and even storms. And yet we know that we are under God's care. We need His help.

The Torah itself tells us to build a *Sukkah*. Long, long ago, after our people left Egypt, they wandered in the wilderness. Because they went from place to place, they could not build regular homes. So they built little huts, or booths, that were open to the sky and wind and rain. Our *Sukkah*, then, reminds us of how our people lived in the wilderness long ago.

Surely we would not choose to live in a *Sukkah* all year. But for one week, a *Sukkah* is wonderful fun.

Sukkot is a holiday of joyous thanksgiving. It is "the time of our happiness." No wonder, then, that some of us think Sukkot is our favorite holiday.

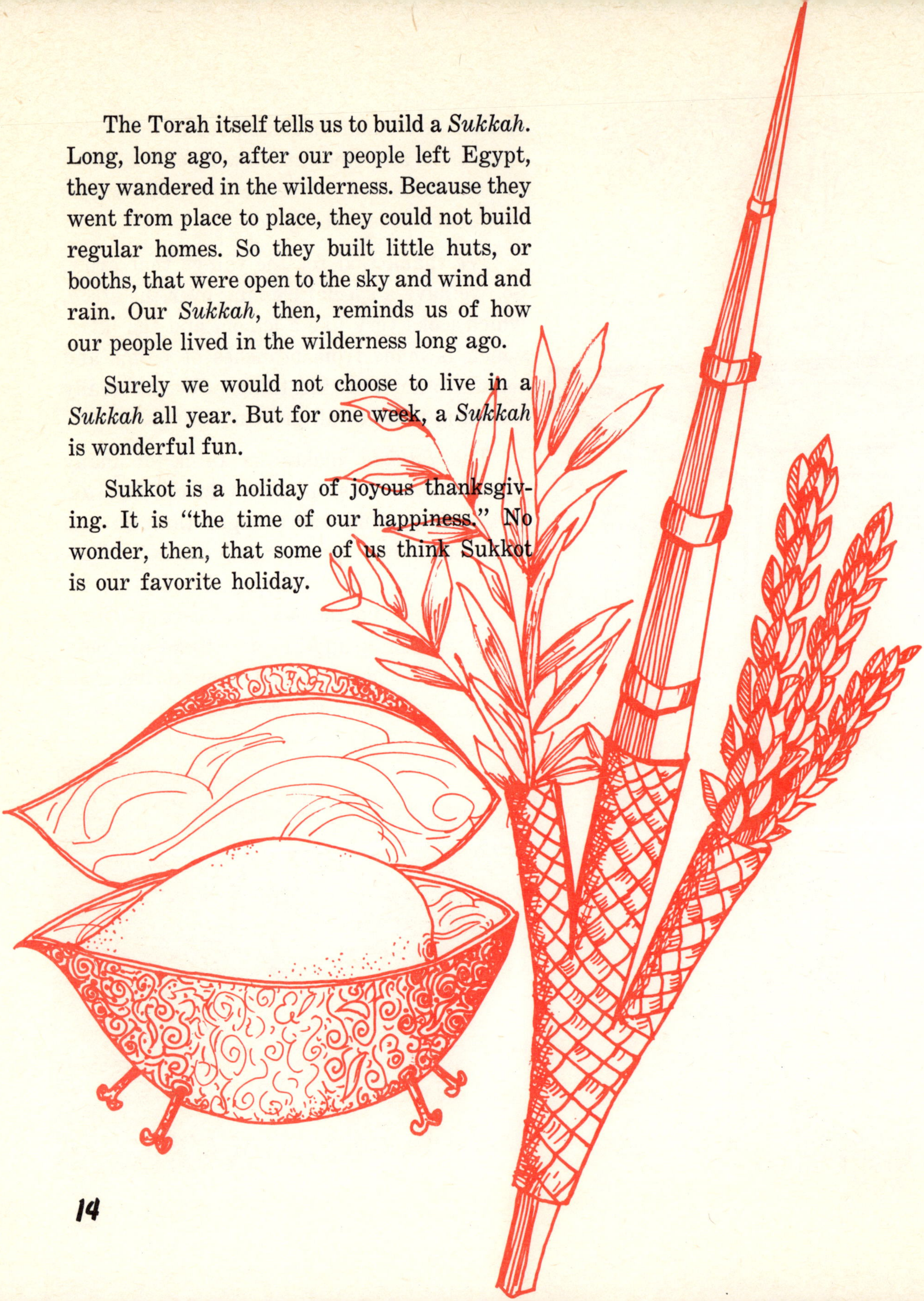

14

4
SIMCHAT TORAH
A PROUD PARADE

'Round and 'round the synagogue,
With love and joy and pride,
The sacred Scrolls we carry show
That Torah is our guide.

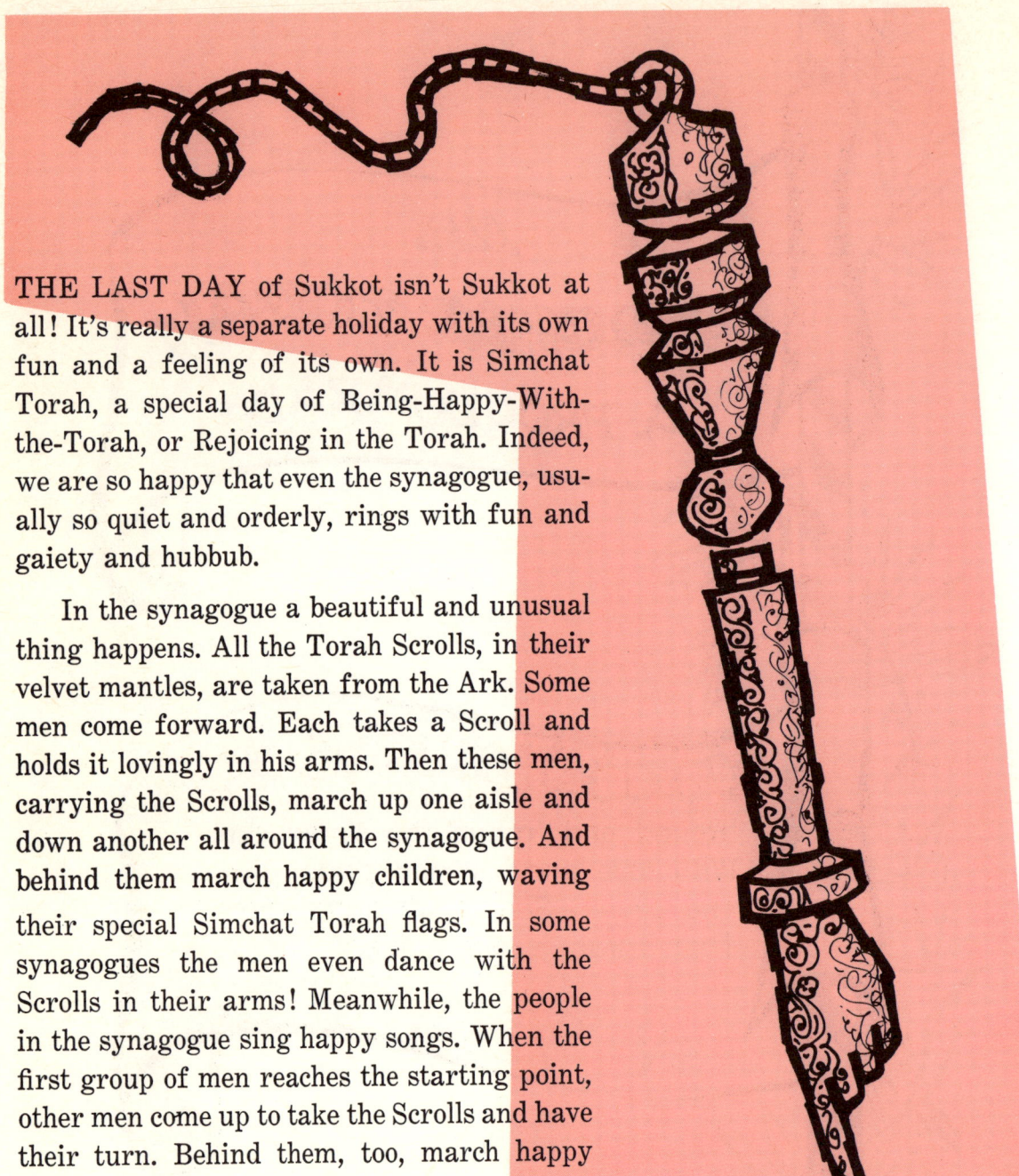

THE LAST DAY of Sukkot isn't Sukkot at all! It's really a separate holiday with its own fun and a feeling of its own. It is Simchat Torah, a special day of Being-Happy-With-the-Torah, or Rejoicing in the Torah. Indeed, we are so happy that even the synagogue, usually so quiet and orderly, rings with fun and gaiety and hubbub.

In the synagogue a beautiful and unusual thing happens. All the Torah Scrolls, in their velvet mantles, are taken from the Ark. Some men come forward. Each takes a Scroll and holds it lovingly in his arms. Then these men, carrying the Scrolls, march up one aisle and down another all around the synagogue. And behind them march happy children, waving their special Simchat Torah flags. In some synagogues the men even dance with the Scrolls in their arms! Meanwhile, the people in the synagogue sing happy songs. When the first group of men reaches the starting point, other men come up to take the Scrolls and have their turn. Behind them, too, march happy children. And this happens seven times. It is a proud parade of people rejoicing in the Torah.

In synagogues all over the world, the Torah is read every week of the year. We start reading at the beginning of the Torah one week. The next week we read the very next part. And so it goes on and on till we come to the end—on Simchat Torah! Then, still on Simchat Torah, we start all over again by reading the beginning of the Torah. So Simchat Torah is a special time for rejoicing with the Torah.

Week after week, all over the world, whether they live in America or Israel or France or Turkey, all Jews read the same part of the Torah. This helps us feel that Jews all over the world belong to each other.

Year after year, we go on reading the Torah. This helps us feel that we belong to Jews who lived in time that is past and also to those who will live in time that is to come.

As long as we read the Torah, week after week and year after year, and as long as we remember what the Torah teaches us, the Jewish people will live on and on and on . . .

We rejoice in the Torah, the treasure of the Jewish people. Simchat Torah is a wonderfully gay and jolly holiday. But it makes us think important and serious thoughts too. It is a holiday with fun of its own and a special feeling of its own. In its own way it is a favorite holiday of the Jew.

5 CHANUKKAH
A WONDERFUL THING HAPPENED THERE

The candles' soft and gentle light
Tells the story of a fight
Our people fought that they might pray
And worship God in their own way.

CHANUKKAH IS A holiday that lasts for eight happy days. Now Chanukkah is not one of the more important Jewish holidays, and yet, in its own way, it is very important.

What makes it so important is a wonderful thing that happened more than twenty-one hundred years ago. At that time the Land of Israel was ruled by the Syrians. The Syrians, in those days, had Greek ideas and the Greek religion. The Syrian king, Antiochus, ordered the Jews to give up the Jewish religion and follow the Greek way. When the Jews refused, Syrian soldiers stormed the Temple in Jerusalem and wantonly destroyed the holy things. The Jews were outraged!

In the little town of Modin there lived an old Jew with his five brave sons. They were called the Maccabees. They gathered the people around them and fought the Syrians. Now the Syrians had many weapons, mighty armies, and huge elephants trained for war. The Jews were surely no match for all this. Still they won the fight, the world's first fight for freedom of religion!

In the Temple there was an oil lamp that was supposed to be lit all the time, day and night. This was the Eternal Light. When the Jews entered the Temple to put it in order, they found that the Eternal Light was no longer lit. They hurried to seek pure oil so that they could light it again. But the Syrians had found the oil and spoiled it! Finally, one

little jug of unspoiled, pure oil was discovered. This was enough oil to keep the lamp burning for only one day. How would they keep the Eternal Light burning?

Then a wonderful thing happened! The oil that was supposed to burn for only one day lasted for eight, till more pure oil was ready! This is why we celebrate Chanukkah for eight days.

On the eight evenings of Chanukkah, we light candles in our homes, one the first night, two the second, and so on until, on the eighth night, all eight candles are lit. And each night there is an extra candle, the *Shamash*, or helper, with which we light the other candles. As we light the candles, the blessings that we say thank God for the wonderful things that happened long ago. The candles burning proudly in the Chanukkah lamp remind us of the glorious fight for freedom of religion.

After the blessings and after the songs, we give Chanukkah *gelt* (money) or Chanukkah gifts. What excitement there is as we tear off the beautiful wrappings and snip away the little bows, blue or white or gold or pink!

Even though Chanukkah reminds us of something very important and serious, the world's first fight for religious freedom, it is a happy holiday full of fun and joy. It is not surprising, then, that many Jews choose Chanukkah as their favorite holiday.

6 TU BISHEVAT
TREES HAVE A HOLIDAY

Each tree we plant in Israel
Is more than just a tree.
The land long dead comes
  back to life
And sets our people free.

DID YOU EVER hear of trees having a New Year? There is a Jewish holiday which is just that! Tu BiShevat is the New Year of the Trees. On this day, many young trees are planted in Israel.

To people living in some parts of the world, like most parts of North America and Europe, this must seem very strange. For it is winter! And winter is surely no time for planting. But in Israel spring has come, and the earth has waked from its winter sleep. Surely, it is a remarkable thing that Jews, no matter where they lived during all these hundreds of years, have always remembered the Land of Israel and its planting time and harvest time. Even though our trees may be covered with a lacy fairyland frost, we remember that in Israel it is a time for planting. We remember that it is time for the New Year of the Trees. So, we celebrate Tu BiShevat.

Long, long ago, when our people lived in the Land of Israel, the land was filled with tall and sturdy cedars, stately cypresses, and many fruit and nut trees—fig and date, olive and almond.

Then, our people was driven from its land, and different rulers came. They paid no attention to the soil and did not take care of the trees. They even chopped them down—carelessly! The growing things withered away. Trees died. Swamps formed, that spread the terrible disease of malaria.

24

When some of the Jewish people returned to the Land of Israel, they wanted to make the land live again. They planted trees—for beauty and for shade from the blistering heat of the sun, for delicious fruits and for wood. They knew that trees help the land and its people in other ways, too. The roots of the eucalyptus tree drink the wetness out of the swamps so that the terrible disease, malaria, is no longer a danger. Other kinds of trees act like a wall to protect the fields of crops, the grapevines, and the fruit orchards from the winds. Trees keep the soil from blowing away. Trees are very important to the land.

We Jews who live outside of Israel want to be part of this wonderful privilege of making the Land of Israel blossom again. We cannot plant the trees ourselves. So, we send money to buy some of the trees that are planted there. We "buy" trees all year, but especially on Tu BiShevat.

In Israel on Tu BiShevat, school children go on hikes and have picnics; they play games and dance and sing songs about trees. But especially they plant trees and have tree-planting ceremonies.

Outside of Israel, Jewish children in religious schools have Tu BiShevat programs too. We eat fruits of the trees that grow in Israel, juicy oranges, sweet dates, and chewy figs. Sometimes even *bokser* or "Johnny Bread," from Israel's carob tree!

All in all, Tu BiShevat is a happy holiday that makes us feel that we too have a part in something very important, building the Land of Israel.

Is this, perhaps, your favorite holiday?

PURIM
·It happened in Persia···

Purim feast and Purim fun!
Oh, the jolly Purim noise!
Story that we love to hear!
Purim, day of many joys!

PURIM IS NOT so holy a holiday as some of the others, but, oh, what fun it is! Like Simchat Torah, it has a jolly feeling, even in the synagogue!

On Purim we hear the *Megillah*, the story of Esther, read in the synagogue.

What a story this book tells! There is a beautiful heroine, Esther, the Jewish girl whom Ahasuerus, king of all Persia, chose to be his queen. There is a hero, Mordecai, Esther's cousin. And there is a villain, the wicked Haman, who was so high and mighty that everyone bowed down to him—everyone except Mordecai.

There is a wicked plot too. Haman, who wanted to get even with Mordecai, the Jew who would not bow, planned to kill all the Jews. But Mordecai, our hero, sent Esther to talk to the king. When Esther told the king that she was Jewish and that Haman planned to kill all the Jews, Ahasuerus had Haman killed instead and all the Jews were saved. So Esther and Mordecai and the Jews of Persia "lived happily ever after."

As the *Megillah* is read, we hiss and boo every time Haman's name is mentioned! We stamp our feet and whirl our *groggers*, the special Purim noise-makers, and make such a racket that Haman's name cannot be heard!

Although all this seems like a television or movie story, for hundreds and hundreds of years hearing the *Megillah* gave our people courage. Over and over again, when enemies arose to harm the Jewish people, our people remembered Haman and thought, "Haman

29

was destroyed, and this new enemy will be destroyed too." The holiday has a message of hope.

This message of hope makes us feel very happy and even jolly. At home, we have a Purim feast. We eat *Hamantashen*, special little three-cornered cakes filled with prunes or poppy seed and honey.

A delightful custom on Purim is the sending of gifts, usually *Hamantashen* and other treats. This is called *Shalach Manot*. Especially, of course, we want to send *Shalach Manot* to the poor. We can do this by giving money to collections which are made for the poor.

Purim is a time for masquerades and carnivals and parties and plays and parades. In Israel, in the city of Tel Aviv, there is a merry parade of floats showing the story of Purim and other stories from the Bible.

Purim is a happy-go-lucky kind of holiday! It is even a time for nonsense! And the fun and noise and nonsense are allowed (and even expected) right in the synagogue as well as at home . . . For hundreds of years, many Jews have considered this merry holiday a favorite. How about you?

8 PESACH
THE TIME OF OUR FREEDOM

The Pesach message that we read:
From Egypt's bondage we were freed.
And freedom now, like freedom then,
Is God's own plan, His gift to men.
When God made man, He made him free,
And that is how man ought to be.

WHEN GROWING THINGS begin to peek through the earth in the Land of Israel and change the color of fields and gardens from a drab, dreary brown to a wide-awake, cheerful green, it is time for Pesach. Outdoors the air itself smells like Pesach, washed and clear and pure—and green! It is spring and a time of freedom. The earth is freed and wakes from the deep sleep of winter. People, too, have the feeling of being freed from winter. There is a feeling of joy in just being alive. It is a time of joy and freedom.

For the Jewish people, the holiday of Pesach is especially "the time of our freedom." Long, long ago, our people were slaves in the land of Egypt. God sent a great leader, Moses, to persuade Pharaoh, the ruler of Egypt, to free the people of Israel. When Pharaoh refused to let the people go, God sent plague after plague upon Egypt. First, all the water turned to blood. The fish in the rivers died.

There was no water to drink. Then came the plague of frogs. There were frogs everywhere, in the fields, in the homes, in the beds, in the food. Plague followed plague. But Pharaoh was stubborn. Finally, when the tenth plague came, Pharaoh had to give in. He ordered the people of Israel to leave immediately!

They left in such a hurry that they had no time to bake their dough into bread. Instead they put the dough onto their shoulders and baked it later. This bread, which did not rise into high, spongy loaves but remained flat and crisp, we call "unleavened bread," or *matzah*. On Pesach when we celebrate the freeing of our people from the slavery of Egypt, we eat no bread, only *matzah*.

Indeed, we are so careful about eating no *chametz* (mainly bread—but some other foods too) on Pesach that we make sure there is no bread, not even a crumb, in the house. Before Pesach, days (and in many homes even weeks)

33

are spent in getting ready for the holiday. Everything is scrubbed and carefully cleaned. The house sparkles! Then, on the night before the holiday, Father searches every room of the house for *chametz*. Carefully, he puts aside every bit of bread he finds, so that he can take the *chametz* outside the next morning and burn it.

Now the house is ready for Pesach. It is here, at home, even more than in the synagogue, that Pesach is celebrated.

9 THE SEDER
THE DINNER THAT IS FOOD FOR THOUGHT

The Seder is a special meal
With prayer and food and song;
And each of these repeats the theme
That slavery is wrong.

FINALLY, PESACH is here! Family and guests sit at the dining-room table for the *Seder*. The *Seder* starts with a service and interesting ceremonies and ends with service and songs. And in between we have what is probably the finest dinner of the whole year.

Each person at the table has a special book, the *Haggadah*, from which to read the *Seder* service.

The service starts with *Kiddush* over the first cup of wine. During the *Seder* we say the blessing for wine four different times, and each time we take a sip.

To remind us of the salty tears our people shed when they were slaves in Egypt, we dip a vegetable into salt water.

In front of Father there is a *Seder* plate with special things on it. There is a bitter herb (*maror*) to remind us of the bitter life our people had when they were slaves in Egypt.

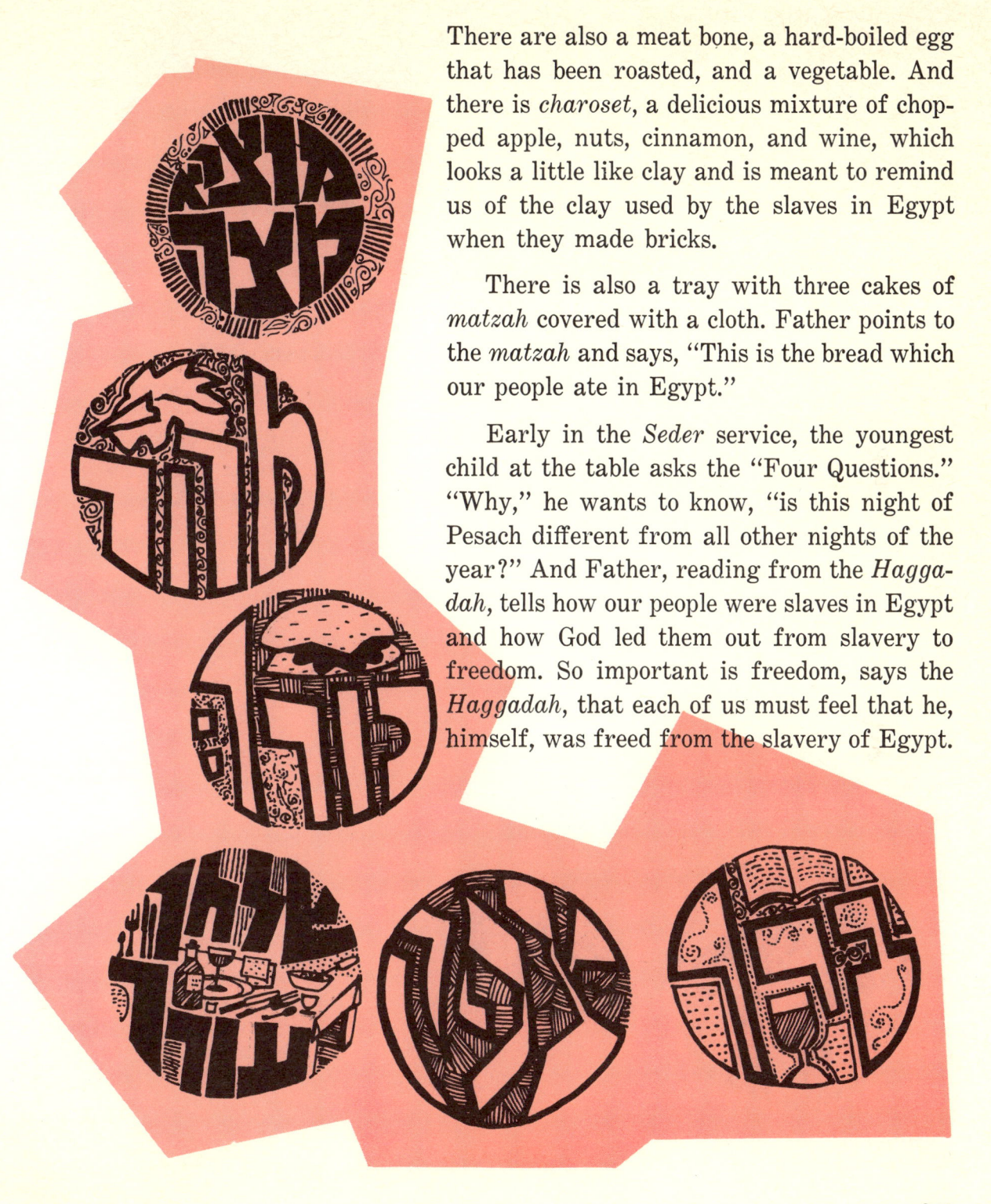

There are also a meat bone, a hard-boiled egg that has been roasted, and a vegetable. And there is *charoset,* a delicious mixture of chopped apple, nuts, cinnamon, and wine, which looks a little like clay and is meant to remind us of the clay used by the slaves in Egypt when they made bricks.

There is also a tray with three cakes of *matzah* covered with a cloth. Father points to the *matzah* and says, "This is the bread which our people ate in Egypt."

Early in the *Seder* service, the youngest child at the table asks the "Four Questions." "Why," he wants to know, "is this night of Pesach different from all other nights of the year?" And Father, reading from the *Haggadah,* tells how our people were slaves in Egypt and how God led them out from slavery to freedom. So important is freedom, says the *Haggadah,* that each of us must feel that he, himself, was freed from the slavery of Egypt.

Father breaks the middle *matzah*, wraps half of it in a napkin and puts it aside. This is the *afikoman*. The children "steal" the *afikoman* and hide it. Dinner over, Father discovers that it is gone. So he offers a prize and gets it back. The little game is over. Everyone eats a small piece of the *afikoman*, and the *Seder* continues.

After dinner, we fill a special cup of wine for the Prophet Elijah, the guest who is never seen but is always imagined at every *Seder*.

Before the *Seder* is over, we sing several jolly songs which tell of the power and the glory of God. And so ends one of the most beautiful evenings of the Jewish year. Most Jews—not all—repeat the *Seder* the next night.

Then Pesach and the eating of *matzah* continue. We realize how precious freedom is, and we thank God for it.

10 ISRAEL INDEPENDENCE DAY
A DREAM COME TRUE

When Israel became a state,
It was a dream come true,
A people's dream, a people's prayer,
A Homeland for the Jew.

OF ALL THE JEWISH holidays, Pesach is the oldest and Israel Independence Day is the newest.

In early times, the People of Israel, the Jewish people, lived in the Land of Israel. Then came mighty nations with powerful armies and drove the People of Israel from the Land of Israel. The Jewish people was scattered all over the world.

Ever since, some Jews have always lived in Israel, but most Jews live in many other countries. And, except for countries where Jews are treated cruelly, we love the countries we live in. But because we are also part of the People of Israel, we have never forgotten the Land of Israel. Our prayers remind us of it every day. And our holidays remind us through the year of the land where our people began.

Less than a hundred years ago, some Jews decided that it was not enough only to pray for the Land of Israel. They decided to try in different ways to work for the land so that it would become a Jewish Homeland. Theodor Herzl worked for the Homeland. Chaim Weizmann worked for the Homeland. Other great men worked for it. And Jews all over the world who were average people, like you and me, worked for it too. Then came a promise that there would be a Jewish Homeland in Palestine, as the Land of Israel was then called. Finally, the United Nations voted to make part of Palestine a Jewish State. The rest was to be Arab. A State of Israel, after two thousand years, was a marvelous thing— a dream come true!

On the other hand, the Arabs in the many large countries around Palestine, were not satisfied to have only part of that land. They wanted it all! The Arabs were furious!

In 1948, Israel declared its independence. Immediately, armies from six Arab nations attacked. For years the Arabs had been killing people in the Jewish settlements of Palestine. Now there was war. The Arab armies were many and mighty. They had powerful weapons. The Jewish army was small and new and without proper weapons. There was little water and less food. The enemy was all around. But the Jewish soldiers were very brave. It was as though two thousand years of hope and prayers and love for the Land of Israel spurred them on. They knew they had to win. And, wonder of wonders, they did win!

The Arab countries, however, were still fiercely angry and refused to make peace. Again and yet again Israel has had to fight the Arabs in order to keep its independence.

Israel, nevertheless, is an independent nation among the nations of the world. Imagine, then, the joy and thankfulness and pride of the people as they celebrate Israel Independence Day with parades and programs, with dancing and singing in streets and fields. And, just as brothers and sisters help celebrate each other's birthdays, so Jews all over the world share the joy and thankfulness and pride of the people of the State of Israel on Israel Independence Day.

11 SHAVUOT

WHEN THE WORLD HELD ITS BREATH

The thunder rolled, the lightning flashed;
The Torah was made known
To teach us that each person's rights
Are precious as our own.

ON THE SECOND day of Pesach, we begin counting the days until we reach forty-nine days, or seven weeks. Then, on the very next day, the fiftieth, we celebrate the holiday of Shavuot, the Feast of Weeks. (Indeed, the Hebrew name *Shavuot* simply means "weeks."

Now we see that Pesach and Shavuot are connected by seven weeks. But there is even more that connects them. Both holidays celebrate harvests in the Land of Israel. Pesach celebrates the early spring harvest. Shavuot celebrates the late spring harvest and is called "The Holiday of the First Fruits" (in Hebrew *Chag HaBikkurim*). For this was the time, in days of old, when our people brought the first fruits of the harvest to the Temple in Jerusalem. And still today, on Shavuot, synagogues and homes are decorated with symbols of spring, green plants and gay flowers.

And there is still another, even more important, connection between Pesach and Shavuot. Pesach celebrates the exodus from Egypt.

After the People of Israel left Egypt, they journeyed in the wilderness until they came to Mt. Sinai. And there a marvelous thing happened! There was thunder and lightning and the loud blast of a horn. Then it seemed as if everything in the world stopped. No breeze blew. No blade of grass stirred. It was as though the world held its breath. And God gave the Ten Commandments and the Torah to the People of Israel.

Pesach is the holiday of freedom; Shavuot is the holiday of "the Giving of the Torah." It was through the Torah that our people learned the true meaning of freedom. For the Torah teaches us how to live with other people. It commands, "Love thy neighbor as thyself." This means that each of us should be fair and kind to all other people, no matter who they are, strong or weak, rich or poor, no matter what their color, whether we know them or not. We should treat them *all* fairly and kindly. We have the right to be free. And all other people have exactly that same right too.

Shavuot is a holiday without very much ceremony; but it is a holiday with a very important message.

Just imagine a world without rules! Just imagine a world without fairness and kindness! Perhaps then we can understand the special meaning of Shavuot.

12. TISHA B'AV
A PEOPLE WEEPS

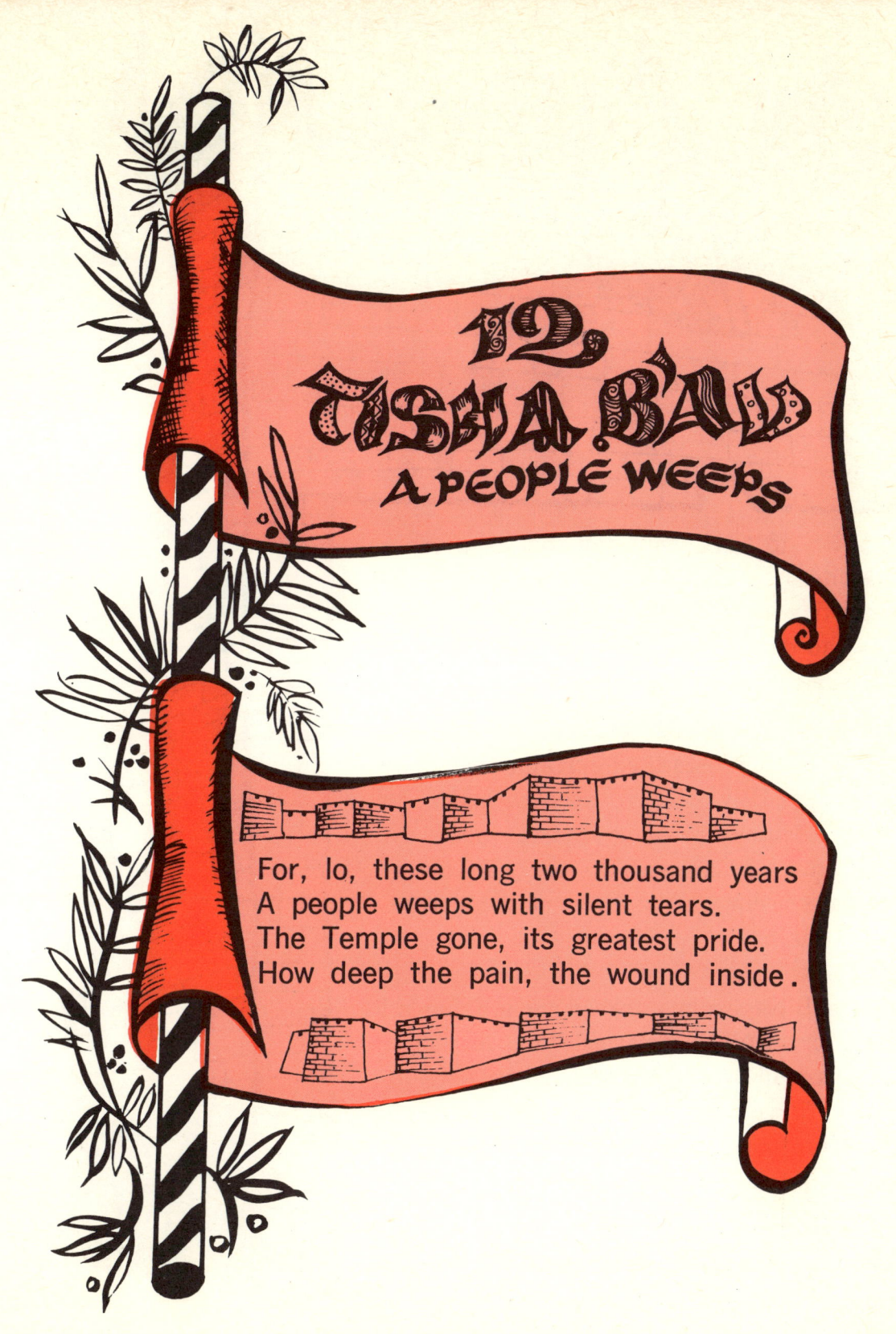

For, lo, these long two thousand years
A people weeps with silent tears.
The Temple gone, its greatest pride.
How deep the pain, the wound inside.

THERE IS ONE holy day that is never a favorite. It is Tishah B'Av, which means the ninth day of the Hebrew month of Av. This is a sad day in the history of our people. It is a day of fasting and sorrowing.

In many synagogues all over the world, the beautifully decorated curtains that hang before the Holy Ark are removed and plain black curtains are hung in their place. At night, many synagogues are dark, lit only by candles or dim lights. In some synagogues people sit on low benches or stools instead of comfortable pews. And everywhere the prayers and Bible readings are sad and are chanted with sorrowful, crying melodies. A people, scattered all over the world, is weeping together. It is a people joined together in expressing the quiet, deep heartache of hundreds and hundreds of years.

Why does a whole people weep? We weep for many things. We weep because it was on this day, about twenty-five hundred years ago, that our Holy Temple in the city of Jerusalem was destroyed by the enemy.

After a time, our people built the Second Temple in the same place. Then, about two thousand years ago, on the same day of the same month, we are told, the Second Temple was destroyed by another powerful enemy nation. And ever since then, our people has been scattered all over the world.

For hundreds of years, many Jews lived happily in Spain. There were Jews who did much to help make Spain one of the important nations of the world in those times. Then, about five hundred years ago, Jews were driven out of Spain. This, too, happened on the ninth day of the month of Av, on Tishah B'Av. Again, this was a sorry day for the Jewish people.

All these unhappy memories make Tishah B'Av a sad, dark day. But then, on the Sabbath that follows Tishah B'Av, during the synagogue services, we read a beautiful message of comfort from the Bible.

And something else comforts us too. True, the Temple is gone. But we are cheered by the fact that after two thousand years, Israel is once again a Jewish state and its capital is the golden, Holy City, Jerusalem.

EPILOGUE

Which Only Means a Few Words Afterwards

*Holidays express the thoughts
Important to the Jew.
Like pictures in a book we read,
They give us pleasure too.*

A MOTHER WAS once asked, "Which of your children is your favorite?" She answered, "Whichever one happens to be with me at the moment."

Perhaps this is the best and truest answer to our question: Which holiday is your favorite? Just as the mother was really saying that *all* her children were favorites, so we feel that all our holidays are favorites, each in its own way. For each holiday has its own meaning, its own importance, its own joys. Each holiday, in turn, as we celebrate it and taste its special flavor, seems to be the favorite.

The Bible tells us, "Be happy on your holiday!" And, indeed, we are!

END

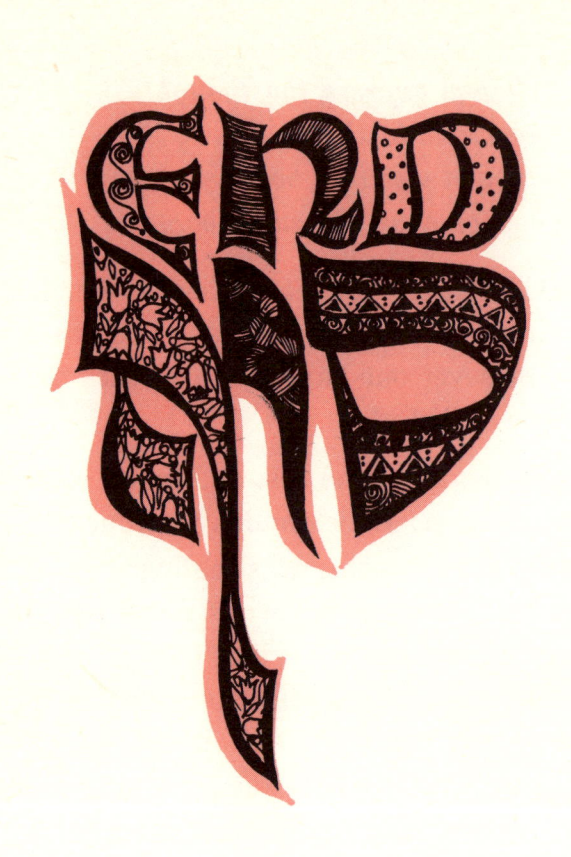